To
Bento

May this story lull you to sleep at ease
and make you dream in peace...

Once upon a time, not too long ago, a beautiful girl,
and a handsome boy fell in love...

They cared so much about each other,
that they decided to spend the rest of
their lives with one another.

They had
a beautiful house
where all their memories
were made around.

As time went by
and their love grew
bigger than the sky,
they realized it was about time
to let someone new
into their lives arrive.

So they began
to fantasize
about another
little

Life.

It took a while
for the stork to stop by.
It got lost quite
a few times.

It was circling,
and circling
day and night.

All the stars of the sky
saw the little stork every night.

One night a shooting star asked:

"Little stork why do you look so sad?"

The little stork started to cry and said:

"Oh beautiful star! I am lost,
but I need to find the way
at all costs!"

"You look very tired"
Said the star,
"Have you come from afar?"

"I come from very far!
My journey is a long distance one,
I was worried
because it was a long way
from home,
and now I am lost
and all alone"

. . . . . . . . . . . . . . . .

"I am tired,
but it will be fine.
I just need to find
the right sign!
I keep on looking
from the immense sky
but it is cloudy sometimes"

"What sign?"
Asked the shooting star?

· · · · · · · · · · · · ·

"The sign that says:
YOU ARE WELCOME TO STOP BY"
Said the little stork.

"I tell my wings to keep on flying

until the magical place we find"

Said the little stork

"All around there is a bright glow
because the place is full of

Love"

"I can help you find the way
that is why our paths crossed along the way"
said the star

"Are you the star the beautiful blue sky calls
destiny?"
Asked the little stork

"Many names are given to me.

Some call me faith, some call me destiny,

others call me luck.

But today, I am your chance to find

The right path!"

"There little stork,
do you see the glow?
That must be the house full of love"

"Thank you star
for showing me
the path.
It was cloudy,
but now I see
that this is the right place
to be"

The house was ready
for the stork to arrive.
The little stork then knocked on the door
and said:

"This wonderful baby
here I was meant to leave

so joy you could feel.

May his life be blessed with

all the love you harvest"

Mom and Dad
then decided
everyone had to know
you had arrived.

It was a feast all around
when everyone saw
your Mommy's belly get
round!

You were welcomed
and blessed,
may life reserve you
only the best!

Into the world
you brought joy
This story is for you
to enjoy!

On

......................................................

into this world you came

and

......................................................

was your name!

The
End

# Acknowledgements

Thank you Jairo for listening to every idea I had. Thank you for your feedback, and for all the improvements I was able to make because you showed me better ways to lay this book out.

Thank you Ale for believing I could do it!

Thank you both for the excitement shown for the making of this story.

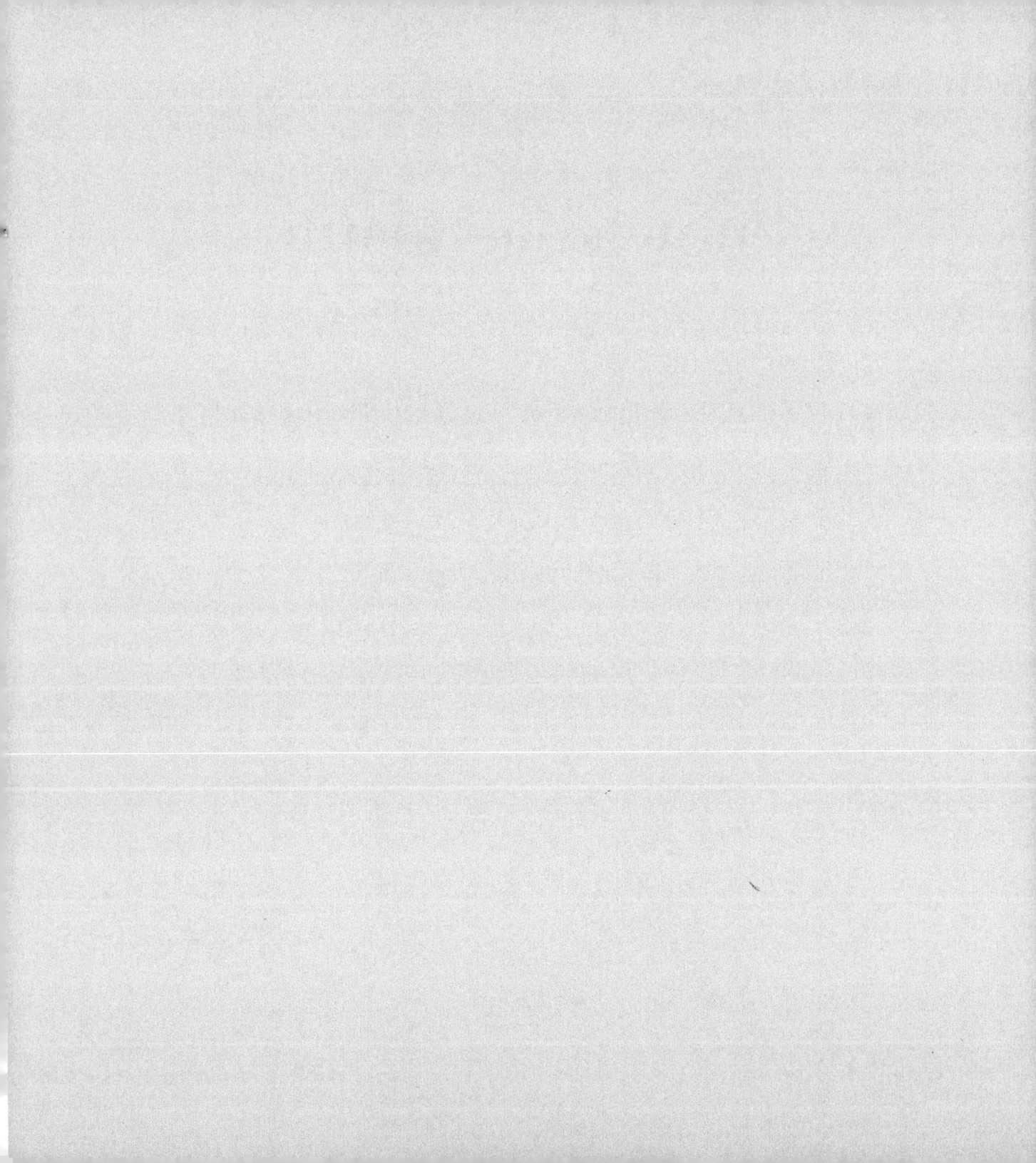

Made in the USA
Las Vegas, NV
18 February 2025